Get Your War On
Comic Strips by David Rees
Introduction by Colson Whitehead

Published by Soft Skull Press
Brooklyn, New York 2002

Get Your War On
©2002 David Rees
Introduction ©2002 Colson Whitehead

First Edition, Second Printing, December 2002
ISBN: 1-887128-76-X

Get Your War On *is not licensed, sponsored, authorized or endorsed by World
Events Productions Ltd., which owns copyright and trademark rights in the
"Voltron" character.*

Design: David Janik | Editorial: Richard Nash

Printed in Canada

Distributed by Publishers Group West
1.800.788.3123 | www.pgw.com

Soft Skull Press, 71 Bond Street, Brooklyn, NY 11217
www.softskull.com

INTRODUCTION by Colson Whitehead

We'd all had quite a shock but people and things were in place to set things right again. That's what they said on television. We had all pretty much agreed that it was going to be okay if we made the appropriate military response. It was all going to be okay. It was okay to send planes because we were sending aid, too. Some sort of surgical strike was necessary to send a message. And we were sending aid, did we mention that we were sending aid to the Afghan people?

But it was kind of awkward when someone said, "We're dropping food aid packages into a country that's one big fucking minefield."

And it was in poor taste when someone said, "It turns the relief effort into a fun game for the Afghan people—a game called 'See if you have any fucking arms left to eat the food we dropped after you step on a landmine trying to retrieve it.'"

And it was a bit off-color to say, "Or maybe they could play, 'See if, when you step on the landmine, the food package flies into your fucking decapitated head as it sails through the air.'"

But it was necessary. And funny.

How to sort through the contradictory impulses and emotions of those days? Weren't we pretty fond of our humanistic values? We kept them in our wallets so that we could whip them out and show them to people on a second's notice like baby pictures. How then to explain that thirst for revenge—well, not revenge, that word is a bit strong isn't it—instead let's say "thirst for some sort of *appropriate response.*" Weren't we, in halcyon days of yore, skeptical if not downright disdainful of our government? How then to explain how reassuring it was to hear an authoritative voice say that we were going to *send a message.* Hadn't we sort of taken for granted that there was a moral center to the universe? Things were kind of rosy 'round these parts. How then to face the knowledge that things are off-kilter, have always been off-kilter and always will be off-kilter? Off-kilter, as in *fucked up*.

This confusion is all there in the debut of David Rees's *Get Your War On,* in the October 9 edition that started the strip. From panel to panel, our clip-art cousins and doppelgängers veer from wrath to self-loathing, ricochet from manic jingoism to giddy despair. They get high on the idea of carnage and then get down with the whiskey in the bottom drawer of their desks. Whether describing the comic or tragic, their expressions never change. They learn nothing from one installment to the next—in fact only wade deeper into the morass of absurdity, lured in by the latest catastrophic news report. Frozen in ignorance. Paralyzed by helplessness.

Rees's use of clip art is his master stroke. Drawn to capture the universal, this particular batch of clip art achieves merely the generic, with their indefinable everyjobs and indeterminate races. And as Rees supplies their dialogue the generic becomes the pathetic. How better to illustrate the horrific repetition of those days—*how many bodies did they dig up, how many bombs did we drop down, how many anthrax cases, how many vaccinations are we short*—than to have these representative citizens re-enact the same poses again and again, mouth the same platitudes and speculations over and over, without progress or relief.

Of course, Rees's characters are more than cookie-cutter people uttering cookie-cutter phrases: they are numb like us. The first strip in *Get Your War On,* the story goes, is a transcription of a conversation Rees had with a friend. Along with many of their neighbors, Rees and his pal had retreated into language. *Relief Effort*, *Heightened Awareness*, *Enduring Freedom*—these were the syllables we used to keep the world at bay. Like George Carlin with a modem, David Rees has a knack for pointing out how we abuse words, distort and torture them toward petty ends. In *Get Your War On,* the languages of different worlds and cultures collide, pile up on each other, and stop meaning for miles in every direction. The slang of hip hop kids strides forth through television and radio, the bloodless inanities of politics trickle down through teleprompters and talking heads, and this sentence is born: "Operation: Enduring Freedom is in the house!" And this sentence makes sense to us, we recognize this monstrosity as our own. *Yeah, Boy-eee!* Inner despair is at odds with outer, workplace persona, forcing private faces into public worlds, and coworkers say things like, "If you want me to hand over that planning report you're more than welcome to bomb my cubicle. Who gives a shit anymore?" Let us look back fondly upon the days of "Take this job and shove it," relic of a happier time. Having the energy to tell your boss to fuck off implies some sort of agency, a little optimism that the world can change for the better.

Rec room, board room, war room, news room—it does not matter, they all rely the same useless phrases. What we see and appreciate in *Get Your War On* is David Rees's attempt to make the words work again —make us accountable for our avoidances, our ellipses. As the link to his website was passed on, e-mail by e-mail, his comics reinvigorated the community. We had been atomized by television, separated from each other. Isolated first by images of horror, then brainwashed by the latest codewords for brutality, banality and other sorts of human nonsense. Forward this link, pass on this message. It will make you smile. Shit is pretty fucked up at the moment, the e-mails said, but at least we are not alone. It's called comfort. Take it where you can get it.

For Chris Browning

October 9, 2001

October 9, 2001

October 9, 2001

October 9, 2001

October 9, 2001

October 9, 2001

October 9, 2001

October 9, 2001

October 14, 2001

October 14, 2001

October 14, 2001

October 14, 2001

October 14, 2001

October 14, 2001

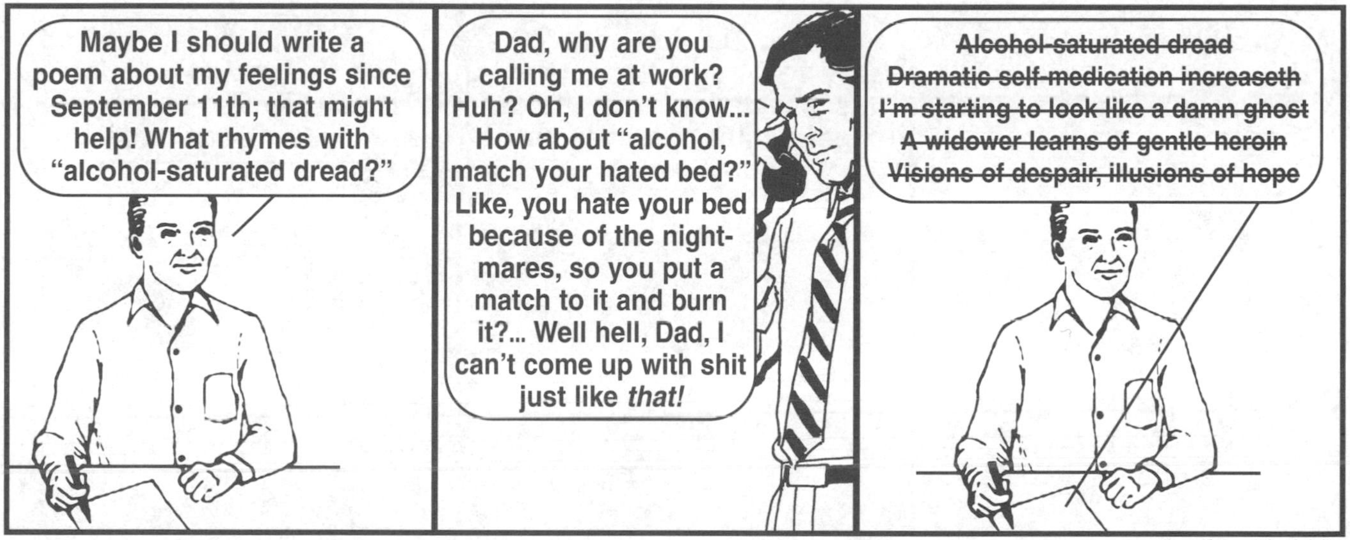

October 30, 2001

October 14, 2001

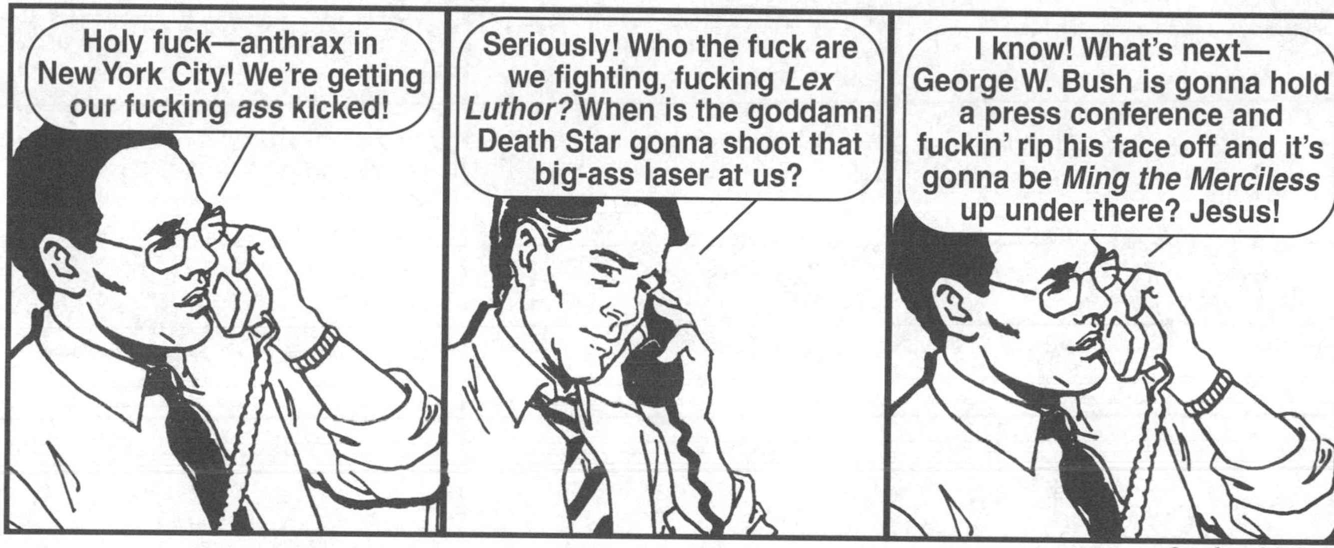

October 14, 2001

October 14, 2001

October 30, 2001

October 30 , 2001

October 30, 2001

October 30, 2001

October 30, 2001

October 30, 2001

October 30, 2001

October 30, 2001

November 8, 2001

November 8, 2001

November 8, 2001

Man! I like a good stiff *Operation: Enduring Freedom* as much as the next guy, but I've reached my limits of understanding! All of a sudden my fucking mailman is a Hero on the Front Lines of the War Against Terror? My daughter wants to sell cookies to help the people my nephew's been sent to fucking *bomb?* I'm supposed to help the FBI find clues and solve crimes? I'M A CLAIMS ADJUSTER, NOT FUCKING ENCYCLOPEDIA BROWN! Who's in charge of this shit?

Agreed! This is totally Loony Toons—I love that the fate of the world hangs in the balance! Bush is talking about conquering evildoers, yet the CIA *can't fucking translate the evildoers' Arabic voodoo-spells!* The "Office of Homeland Security" makes the DMV look like fucking Delta Force! And, look, I understand why *Osama bin Laden* sounds crazy—he's an eleven-foot-tall motherfucker who lives in a cave! But why does Bush always sound like he's addressing a goddamn Dungeons & Dragons convention? At least I can tear my hair out full-time since I've been laid off!

November 8, 2001

November 29, 2001

November 29, 2001

November 29, 2001

November 29, 2001

November 29, 2001

December 12, 2001

December 12, 2001

December 12, 2001

December 12, 2001

December 12, 2001

December 12, 2001

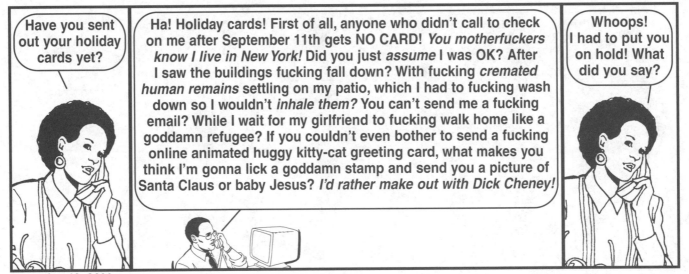

December 12, 2001

December 12, 2001

January 17, 2002

January 17, 2002

January 17, 2002

January 17, 2002

February 18, 2002

February 18, 2002

February 18, 2002

February 18, 2002

February 18, 2002

February 18, 2002

February 18, 2002

March 28, 2002

March 28, 2002

March 28, 2002

April 22, 2002

April 22, 2002

April 22, 2002

April 22, 2002

May 2, 2002

May 2, 2002

May 2, 2002

May 2, 2002

May 2, 2002

May 2, 2002

May 22, 2002

May 22, 2002

May 22, 2002

May 22, 2002

May 22, 2002

Summer, 2002

July 11, 2002

July 11, 2002

July 11, 2002

July 11, 2002

July 11, 2002

July 11, 2002

July 11, 2002

August 7, 2002

August 7, 2002

August 7, 2002

August 7, 2002

August 7, 2002

August 7, 2002

August 7, 2002

August 7, 2002

March 28, 2002

August 18, 2002

Adopt-A-Minefield

The Adopt-A-Minefield Campaign engages individuals, community groups, and businesses in the United Nations effort to remove landmines around the world. The Campaign helps save lives by raising funds to clear minefields and by raising awareness about the global landmine crisis. The idea behind Adopt-A-Minefield is both powerful and simple. Designed to move beyond the political and policy debates typically associated with banning the use of landmines, the Campaign provides a practical solution to ridding the world of the **more than 70 million mines** that contaminate it.

The **hundreds of thousands of landmine survivors** worldwide bear witness to the indiscriminate nature of antipersonnel mines. While **a mine can cost as little as $3 to produce, it can cost up to $1000 to disable.** Local communities in mine-affected countries often do not have the resources to clear their own land. They typically depend upon financial assistance from governments and international organizations. Adopt-A-Minefield is a grassroots effort to provide this aid.

Afghanistan and *Get Your War On*

It is estimated that up to 300 Afghans are injured or killed by landmines every month—the highest rate in the world. Many cases go unreported because the injured do not have access to medical care. Landmines also pose a direct threat to economic recovery. More than 800 km^2 of residential area, commercial land, roads, irrigation systems, and primary production land are littered with mines and unexploded ordnance.

Your purchase of *Get Your War On* will help support the work of Mine Detection & Dog Center Team #5 in the Western region of Afghanistan. The author is donating all the royalties, and Soft Skull Press is contributing an additional percentage of sales to the campaign. You are providing the first and vital steps toward reconstruction.